Ripley Readers

Horses

*All true and
unbelievable!*

RIPLEY
PUBLISHING

a Jim Pattison Company

Do you know how to ride a horse?

Some horses run fast, and some can jump over hurdles!

A racehorse has a friend to help him. He is called a lead pony.

See them walking side by side?

Big draft horses work around a farm.

Some horses have a lot of fur
so they will not get cold.

A little horse is called a pony.

Look at that funny horse with hair on its lip!

Horses like to walk
around and eat grass.

A horse can eat from
sun up to sun down!

Do you like to eat food that is sweet? So do horses!

They will spit out food
they do not like.

You can see how old a horse is from its teeth.

The oldest horse was 62 years old!

Just like we have to clip our nails, horses have to trim their hooves!

The part under a horse's hoof is called a *frog*.

Different horses have
different names.

A baby horse is a foal.
A girl horse is a mare.
A boy horse is a stallion.

Horses come in many colors: brown, black, white, or gray.

Did you know a horse can get a sunburn?

Horses are good at seeing in
the dark.

They can see better at night than we can!

A horse can sleep down on its side or up on its feet!

Do you think you could sleep standing up?

A zorse has a horse mom and a zebra dad!

See the black and white stripes on its legs?

Horses live all over the world!

Is there one that you like the best?

RIPLEY Readers

All true and unbelievable!

Ready for More?

Ripley Readers feature unbelievable but true facts and stories!

LEVEL ONE — Sounding it out

LEVEL TWO — Reading with help

LEVEL THREE — Independent reading

LEVEL FOUR — Chapters

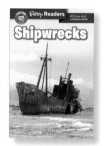

Look for Ripley Readers on Amazon.com!